WORLD OF WONDER

Published by Creative Education
123 South Broad Street
Mankato, Minnesota 56001

Creative Education is an imprint of
The Creative Company.

Art direction by Rita Marshall
Design by The Design Lab
Editorial assistance by Dr. Christopher Rose
Photographs by The Image Finders (Ernesto Burciaga, Dan
Tyrpak), Jay Ireland & Georgienne Bradley/
Bradleyireland.com, JLM Visuals (Richard P. Jacobs, Breck P.
Kent, Alex Kerstitch), KAC Productions (Larry Ditto, John &
Gloria Tveten), Robert McCaw, McDonald Wildlife
Photography (Joe McDonald), James P. Rowan, Simpson
Nature Photography (Gary W. Sargent, Ann & Rob
Simpson), Tom Stack & Associates (J. Lotter Gurling, Kitchin
& Hurst, Ed Robinson, Tom & Therisa Stack)

Library of Congress Cataloging-in-Publication Data

Hoff, Mary King.
Metamorphosis / by Mary Hoff.
p. cm. — (World of wonder)
Summary: Discusses metamorphosis, describing how various
animals change from one form to another as they grow.
ISBN 1-58341-268-9
1. Metamorphosis—Juvenile literature. [1. Metamorphosis.]
I. Title. II. World of wonder (Mankato, Minn.)

QL981 .H64   2003
571.8'76—dc21   2002034934

First Edition

9 8 7 6 5 4 3 2 1

cover & page 1: monarch caterpillar and butterfly
page 2: a barnacle
page 3: a mature bullfrog

ative Education presents

WORLD OF WONDER

METAMORPHOSIS

BY MARY HOFF

Tadpoles that turn into frogs 🌿 Little grubs that become flying beetles 🐈 Swimming blobs that develop starfish arms ❄ The world is full of animals that change from one form to another as they grow. Some start with fish-like gills and end up breathing with lungs. Some grow legs. Some sprout wings.

🌍

THIS TYPE OF MAJOR CHANGE is called metamorphosis. It occurs in many kinds of animals, including insects, fish, amphibians, and mollusks. No matter what shape the changes may take, all are **adaptations** that help animals survive and pass life on to another generation.

Butterflies are famous for their shape-shifting

WHY CHANGE?

Having very different life stages helps animals in many ways. One is by reducing competition among members of the same **species**. Tadpoles, which are juvenile frogs, live in the water and eat mainly algae and plants. Frogs live on land and eat insects and other small animals. As a result, frogs don't compete with their own young for the resources they need.

☞ Another advantage of metamorphosis is that it allows

animals to excel at different things in different life stages. A caterpillar has a mouth and digestive system that allow it to do lots of eating—just the thing for the "growing" phase of life. When it turns into a butterfly, it isn't as well-equipped for eating, but it has wings that can carry it long distances to search for a mate and a place to lay eggs.

✳ In many ocean animals that metamorphose, the younger stage is the "moving about" stage. The larvae of

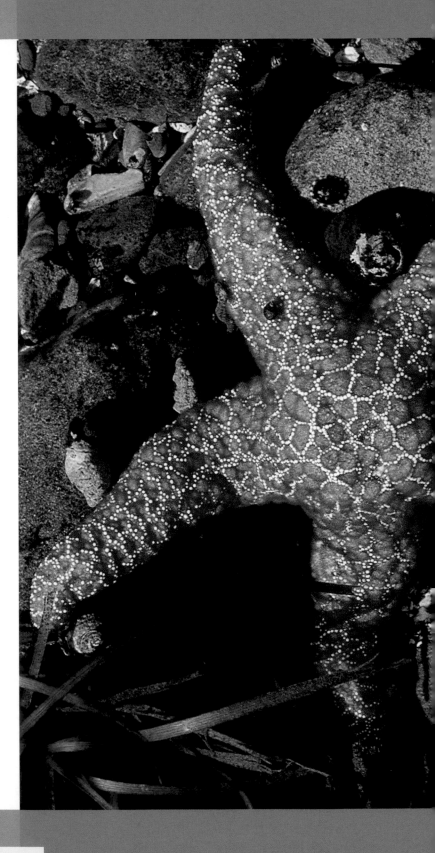

starfish and sea anemones can travel long distances through the water. When it's time to transform into adults, they change shape and settle into one place.

NATURE NOTE: *The larvae of corals—animals that build coral reefs—may travel more than 10 miles (16 km) before metamorphosing into stationary adults.*

DISSOLVING INSECTS

A monarch caterpillar hatches from an egg. It eats and grows, then **molts** when its skin gets too tight. When it is between one and two weeks old, it attaches by one end to the underside of a leaf and turns into a pupa. Inside the pupa's covering, the caterpillar starts to dissolve. Clusters of cells called imaginal discs grow—

NATURE NOTE: *Some insect larvae form a cocoon—a covering of silk or other protective material—around themselves before they change into pupae.*

feeding on the dead caterpillar cells—and form an insect with long legs and colorful wings. After about 10 days, the covering splits and a monarch butterfly emerges.

In insects, change that involves a larva, pupa, and adult is known as complete, or holometabolous, metamorphosis. The adults of insects that go through this kind of change are very different from the larvae that hatch from eggs.

A newly hatched butterfly stretches its wings

☀ Insects that undergo complete metamorphosis include moths, beetles, ants, wasps, butterflies, bees, and flies. Sometimes the larvae have special names. Butterfly and moth larvae are called caterpillars. Beetle larvae are called grubs. The crawling larvae of flies are called maggots.

NATURE NOTE: *At one point during butterfly metamorphosis, the contents of the pupa may be mostly liquid.*

The young of beetles are known as grubs

OTHER INSECTS

Some insects, such as springtails and silverfish, are ametabolous—which means they don't metamorphose. Others, such as grasshoppers, cockroaches, dragonflies, and stoneflies, go through a process called hemimetabolous (incomplete) metamorphosis. The young of these insects are called nymphs. They tend to look a lot like the adults. Their metamorphosis con-

NATURE NOTE: *The black fly or buffalo gnat, an insect found in many parts of the world, forms its pupa underwater. When the adult emerges, it rides an air bubble to the water's surface.*

These grasshopper nymphs look like small adults

sists of growing and adding body parts such as wings, but not of radical change. They molt as they grow larger but do not form pupae. ✳ The nymphs of dragonflies, damselflies, mayflies, and stoneflies live in water, breathing through gills. Sometimes these nymphs are called naiads. Adults emerge from the naiads' last molt with wings and lungs that enable them to live out of water.

NATURE NOTE: *Some mayflies live only a few hours after metamorphosis is complete.*

MUSSEL MORPHING

Freshwater mussels, clam-like creatures that live in rivers and lakes, might not look like they could travel very far. But they do—as larvae called glochidia. Mother mussels release the microscopic glochidia into the water. Some of these young come in contact with the gills of fish. They stick to the gills and get nourishment from the fish. Mussel

NATURE NOTE: *Mussel larvae, or glochidia, die unless they find a fish to ride within a few days.*

15

Glochidia hitch a ride on fish soon after birth

glochidia can travel long distances attached to a swimming fish.

✤ While traveling with the fish, the glochidia undergo metamorphosis. They develop internal organs, such as a heart and digestive tract. Then, after a couple of weeks, they drop off and sink to the bottom. They stay in their new location for the rest of their lives.

NATURE NOTE: *Female mussels can produce millions of glochidia in a single year.*

SETTLING IN

Many **invertebrates** that live at the bottom of the sea have on-the-go larvae. Adult sand dollars creep along on tiny spines that stick out from their bodies. You would think they would have a hard time avoiding overcrowding as they multiply. But they don't. That's because they and other **echinoderms** produce swimming larvae. The larvae travel to new locations, then metamorphose into bottom-dwelling adults.

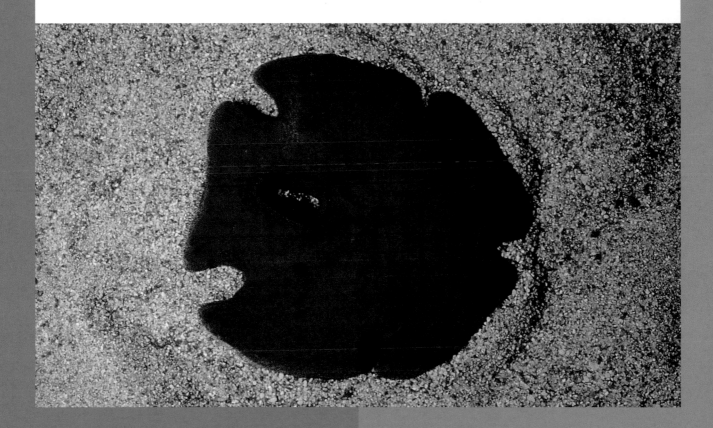

Sand dollars swim as larvae and crawl as adults

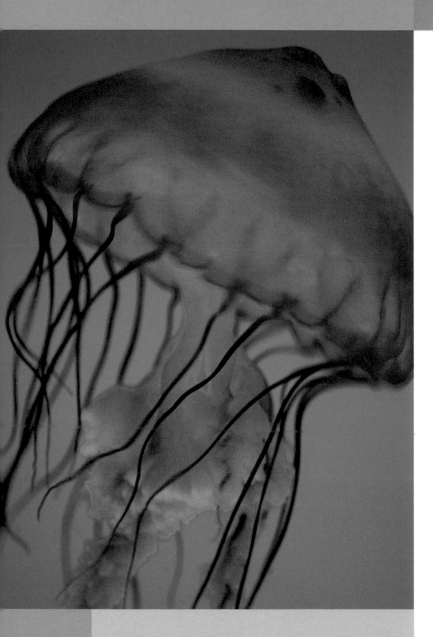

NATURE NOTE: *The larvae of barnacles, shellfish that attach themselves to boats and other underwater surfaces, tend to settle around other barnacles, attracted by a special barnacle chemical.*

◆ Cnidarians are a group of ocean-going animals that includes jellyfish, corals, and sea anemones. Their larvae are called planulae. Planulae have tiny hairs called cilia on their bodies that help them travel through the water. They metamorphose into adults when they get a cue from their environment, such as the presence of a certain chemical in the water. Scientists think this helps ensure that the place in which they settle can meet their physical needs.

TRANSFORMING TADPOLES

Some **vertebrates** metamorphose, too. In early spring, a frog lays her eggs in a pond. The young that emerge are called tadpoles. They look nothing like their parents. They have tails instead of legs, and they breathe with gills instead of lungs.

☾ Gradually, the tadpoles change. Their gills, tail, and teeth disappear. They grow legs.

NATURE NOTE: *Paradoxical frog tadpoles, found in South America, can grow to be 10 inches (25 cm) long.*

In a few months' time, this will be a wood frog

Their ears, eyes, mouth, respiratory system, digestive system, and color change. They switch from eating plants to eating insects. They become adult frogs. The time it takes to go from egg to adult varies with the species and weather. Some tadpoles metamorphose in less than a month. Others spend the winter as tadpoles.

☀ Frogs and toads are members of a group of animals called amphibians. Other members of this group, such as most salamanders, undergo metamorpho-

sis, too. The red-spotted newt of North America, a kind of salamander, starts life in the water. After metamorphosis, it lives on land. After a couple of years, it matures and returns to the water to breed.

NATURE NOTE: *The nymphs of some species of periodical cicadas, an insect found in North America, live underground for 17 years before they metamorphose into adults.*

FISH CHANGE

Flounders are flat fish that lie on the ocean floor. Their eggs hatch into tiny larvae. When they have grown about one-half inch (13 mm) long, the larvae flatten out. One eye moves so that both eyes are on the same side of the face. As a result, the grown flounder can lie on the ocean bottom without losing the use of one eye.

❄ The sea lamprey is another fish that undergoes an interesting metamorphosis. Worm-like sea lamprey larvae burrow into the rocky bottom of streams. They

The flat flounder blends into the ocean floor

stay there for years with their mouths exposed, catching food that floats by.

Then they start to metamorphose. Their eyes grow larger, and they develop a

suction-cup-like mouth. They turn from brown to gray and white. They swim

downstream to the ocean or a lake, where they survive by attaching their

mouths to other fish and sucking blood from them.

NATURE NOTE: *In most flounders, both eyes are on the right side after metamorphosis. In some other flatfish, they end up on the left side instead.*

Sea lampreys become parasites when grown

❧ The o'opu nopili, a Hawaiian fish, hatches in streams. The larvae go out to sea and live there for several months. Then they travel back inland. When they come to a waterfall, they stop and metamorphose. Their mouths move to the bottom of their bodies, and they develop a fat lip. When they are done changing, the fish continue their journey upstream, using their transformed mouth like a suction cup to climb rocks up the waterfall.

A look at the sea lamprey's suction-cup mouth

CONTROLLING METAMORPHOSIS

What makes a caterpillar form a pupa, a tadpole grow legs, and a flounder's eye move? The signals to undergo such changes are carried by substances within the animals' bodies called **hormones**.

✳ Scientists have conducted many experiments to learn how hormones control

NATURE NOTE: *The warmer the weather, the faster caterpillars turn into butterflies.*

As larvae, dogbane beetles live in the soil

metamorphosis. One scientist discovered that hormones produced in a moth's head are important to metamorphosis by cutting a pupa in half and observing that only the head half metamorphosed. Others have shown that tadpoles metamorphose sooner if exposed to a chemical element called iodine. This suggests that hormones from the **thyroid gland** influence amphibian metamorphosis. In insects, structures called corpora allata, found near the brain, secrete a hormone that prevents

larvae from metamorphosing. When the brain tells the corpora allata to stop producing this hormone, metamorphosis begins.

☼ Timing is important in metamorphosis. If a caterpillar turned into a pupa before it finished growing, the butterfly might not be big enough to successfully reproduce. If a sea anemone dropped to the ocean floor in an undesirable habitat, it might not survive.

❋ What determines the timing of metamorphosis? Animals have inside them a sense of time

that is like a clock telling their bodies when to do certain things. That sense, combined with factors such as temperature and the amount of sunlight, tells various parts of the body when to produce hormones, and other parts of the body when to pay attention to hormones. There are still many questions to be answered when it comes to understanding how metamorphosis is regulated.

NATURE NOTE: *Scientists have found that tadpoles metamorphose sooner if the body of water they are in is drying up.*

Grown cypress beetles can be tree-eating pests

AMAZING ADAPTATIONS

From caterpillars that become bright butterflies to tadpoles that turn into frogs, many animals undergo dramatic changes in their form and function as a way to meet the challenge of finding the food, mates, and desirable living places they need to survive and reproduce.

❄ The ability to metamorphose is just one of countless adaptations that help living things thrive in the challenging world around them. They are valuable reminders of how intricately the lives of various creatures are intertwined. As humans make changes that affect the environment, it's important to remember and respect these connections. In doing so, we can help ensure the future health and beauty of this amazing world, this world of wonder.

NATURE NOTE: *Some starfish are smaller than this "o" when they undergo metamorphosis.*

WORDS TO KNOW

Adaptations *are characteristics that contribute to a living thing's ability to survive or reproduce.*

Echinoderms *are members of a group of ocean-going animals that includes sea stars, sea urchins, and sand dollars.*

Hormones *are chemical messengers that travel through a living thing, coordinating functions among various parts of the body.*

Invertebrates *are animals without backbones.*

The young of animals that undergo metamorphosis are called **larvae***.*

An insect **molts**—*sheds its outer, too-tight skin—as it grows.*

A **pupa** *is a form some insects take as they transform from larva to adult.*

A **species** *is a group of living things that can successfully breed with each other.*

The **thyroid gland** *is a part of the body that releases hormones that regulate growth.*

Vertebrates *are animals with backbones.*

INDEX